GHOST MATINEE

POEMS

CATHRYN SHEA

Attention schools and businesses: for discounted copies on large
orders, please contact the publisher directly.

For information contact:
Unsolicited Press
Portland, Oregon
www.unsolicitedpress.com
orders@unsolicitedpress.com
619-354-8005

Cover Design: Kathryn Gerhardt
Editor: S. Stewart
ISBN: 978-1-963115-33-8

Table of Contents

I. GOOD ENOUGH

II. KNOW THE DAHLIAS

III. EVERY BIT OF IT MINE

Acknowledgments

My thanks to the editors and staff of the following magazines where these poems first appeared, sometimes in a different version:

Amythyst Review "*Thin Places & Sacred Spaces*" anthology, July 2024, "Display of Phalaenopsis Orchids"

Arboreal Literary Magazine, May 2023, "Please Give Me Your Ars"

Assisi: An Online Journal of Arts & Letters, Summer 2021, "Blessed Be the Calving" and "Mutual Denominator"

The Aurorean, Summer/Fall 2020 (last issue), "The Social Life of California Poppies"

The BeZine, Ukraine-Peace Special Section, April 2022, "Equipoise," "Dependable," "A [New] Context"

Blue Mountain Review, Summer 2021, "Novel Aloofness"

Chronogram: Hudson Valley Arts, Culture, Spirit, January 2020, "The Slick Slope"

Constellations, A Journal of Poetry and Fiction, Fall 2023, "An American Vernacular"

Eastern Iowa Review, Issue 10, 2020, "In the Wake of My Sister"

Gargoyle Magazine, 2021 and 2025, "Every Bit Mine," and "Biscotti with the Taj Mahal;" "Beyond the Milky Way" and "They Say the Mystery of Antarctica's Sea Ice Has Been Solved"

Gyroscope Review, Fall 2020, "The Academia I Never Had"

Literary Hatchet, Winter 2020, "Watersheds"

Marin Poetry Center Anthology, 2022, "Dependable"

The New Verse News, December 10, 2019, "To My Grandsons in the Future"

ONE ART, August 5, 2020 and February 2024, "Missive to Nancy" and "Anniversary Memento"

Poet Lore, Fall/Winter 2008, "Eyeglasses"

Plum Tree Tavern, May 2023, "Mannequins Yearning for Eye Contact"

Quiddity, Fall/Winter 2009-10, "Good Enough"

Rat's Ass Review, Winter 2020, "I'm Not Really Watching Any News" and "Quarry"

Redheaded Stepchild, Summer 2021, "Dimpled"

Rise Up Review, November 2020, "To-do List During a Pandemic Ignored Because of Protests"

Rust and Moth, 2016, "The Secrets Hidden in a Pear Tree" and "The Kid on Holiday"

San Antonio Review, April 16, 2023, "Love Story of Pears," "The Shades Pulled Up and Down," "Cure Redux," "When Wind Turbine Blades Expire"

The Schuylkill Valley Journal, Summer/Fall 2020 print issue, "Pop Art Supermarket"

Typehouse, January 2019, "The Undercover Activity of Poplars"

"Mutual Denominator" was nominated for Best of the Net 2021.

A few of these poems have appeared in the author's chapbooks in differing forms. "Know the Dahlias" was featured in the *Reverberations Two* project, April 2022 at the Sebastopol Center for the Arts and in the *Reverberations Two* companion art book. This is an exhibition of media artists creating art in response to the poem they are paired with.

GHOST MATINEE

POEMS

CATHRYN SHEA

I.
Good Enough

Please Give Me Your Ars

Sun daubed on a bloody sky,
gauze bandages of clouds.
Season of fires again.
Predictable each year now
and on schedule,
part of a new narration for autumn.
Bad air fitted with particulate matter
seeps into my lungs for the long haul.
The sunset is grim
with evacuations out on the coast
and claret-red inland where wineries sear,
vineyards with grapes burned at the stake.
I lapse into a dead language,
a wounded soliloquy
reaching out like arms of a nebula.
Salva nos, something far away repeats
like an irksome tune
when all I want to behold is art, beauty.
Our tomorrows prance around the kitchen table
with its legion of empty chairs
and stacks of newsprint
where food should be served.
But we eat in front of the TV,
our minds flickering, snowy and lacy.
I witness world events that require a dictionary
vaster than my galaxy. No wonder
what I hold feels obscure and I despair
of convincing anyone these warnings are dire.

Blood Beloved

1.

Beloveds have escaped from the basement;
you can't even see the stitching
that sewed the remains
of my ancestors together.

I did not shriek or rend my clothes,
enigma tucked between my legs.
The clues of one side of my ancestry
on the wall in curlicue frames arranged just so

to stare back at progeny—
how I miss them, their neglected graves
far-flung as they are near suffering oaks,
ribs of stone underneath.

Their realia, objects from everyday
help me grasp the past, open
a portal to them when I hold
the stuff of their lives.

My own guts built of their DNA,
spectral and waiting, in stories
forever hunting deer,
forever fishing trout,

setting a table for the deep-dish pie.
My cabinet full of knick-knacks,
relics from those lives:
a complete set of bone china,

including a gravy boat, untouched for years,
salt and pepper shakers in the shape
of two googly-eyed pups hugging
amid psalms on wedding invitations,

the silver-plated butter dish with its
ingenious pocket for ice under the cut crystal,
covered with a domed lid like a courthouse roof,
and with its blunt knife seated in the broken cradle.

Summers, my orphaned teenage grandmother
(who was raised by her sister) would hurry
bearing heirloom butterdish from the icehouse
to the ranch house dining table with haste

yet still the butter would melt.
Her brother-in-law back in from the field,
he would flop on the floor
in his clammy coveralls, kick off grassy boots,

stretch out his legs, and he'd play
with the dog, a little terrier, finally
go wash up, come back to the table
in clean undershirt to eat supper.

My cabinet is full
of leftovers from that ranch
where my mother and uncle played,
full of bric-a-brac, personal effects

that were used every day:
the nesting stoneware pots, their flat lids
glazed with irises, crazed
from the wood-burning oven.

Years of recipes (some published
in the San Joaquin County cookbook):
side dishes of scalloped potatoes,
broccoli au gratin, macaroni and fontina.

The gilt swell of sunset with its still
air and insect choruses—
perhaps swallows would emerge back then
to feast and loop in boundless figure eights.

The ranch lost, mortgaged to a spooky banker
long since buried. Family
ends up moving to town, relocating
as best they could into a little stucco house

with modern amenities
like indoor plumbing,
a gas stove, icebox, and the piano
that my aunt would play

(who was really my first cousin once removed)
with keys like baby teeth,
keys to unlocking the cosmos
of that part of my maternal past.

2.

The children of my children
at my knees now
wallowing, poking, tugging,
making shrill animal noises.

Cereal bowls half full of warm milk,
ripe bananas, crushed graham crackers

dotted around the living space—
better to give them a trough—

floor dense with Legos
and action figures and projectiles
from plastic guns and unidentifiable parts
scattered just so to inflict calamitous pain on feet.

And Pokémon cards,
but these are sacred
so they are organized and neatly kept
in albums, instead of family photos.

These children of my children, my fortune,
run to me when I visit. Jump up and down
on the couch, launch themselves into my arms.
They are in me and I am in them, adored.

Dearest creatures, my beloved blood
from a galaxy of nebulous deeds,
beings magnetic and malleable,
you are the result of bygone pleasures and chance.

Good Enough

Drive out past the misplaced rice paddies
that love autumn burns and think they're in China,
past the slough where carp cruise
their own rendition of Asia, except those Jet Skis
obscure their vision. Go beyond the longest finger of Delta
flipping the bird at the hazy sky
particulate in the dawn of another blazing day—

At the local flea market there's a stall
which you won't find without a map of this shutdown town
whose name nobody remembers.
It's not that place where they sell copycat
Pradas, LVs, and Kate Spades—people here don't know
these fancy labels, would trash them anyway—

Behind that corroded Suburban,
see all the folding tables straining under salty, red
rocks from Mars, jars of spilled
crude from Exxon Valdez mixed with Captain Hazelwood's
farewell Yukon Jack. There are the bones
preserved in lava of Harry R. Truman, eternal proprietor
of Mount St. Helens Lodge
alongside wholesale ash from his wife, fair Loowit.

You'll find depleted uranium
sealed in tiny canisters from Farallon Islands resting
by urns filled with water from the Mississippi
cancer corridor, vials of rust from nails once bloodied
with stigmata from Calvary, mostly crucified
petty thieves. You'll need to compete with crowds

20

crushed around signs
painted sloppily "Extirpated Families," "Extinct Species"
to see the miracles:

wayside aster, purple poking through silt from the dam;
the lined pocketbook (*lampsilis binominata*)
by no means a wallet clam;
the passenger pigeon (with its own passenger mite), legendary
for having unwittingly fed the poor and indentured.
And a small fish named after a slave boat,
the *Amistad gambusia*, known only to occur
in Goodenough Spring (pronounced *good enough*), a tributary
buried under sludge near the Rio Grande.
All these creatures on the verge of rebirth.

Pop Art Super Market

What would it feel like to squeeze
the Wonder Bread? Squish the Twinkies?
Stack tomato soup to the ceiling?
The next time I go for groceries
I'll install in my brain no detection of logic—
Like a six-year-old before the age of reason,
I'll be dazzled by neon colors,
repetition of shapes, hilarious gibberish.
The cuteness of fish, cheese, eggs,
rainbows of produce.
I won't ask where pork chops come from.
All cereal boxes bright toys
to be thrown on the floor,
chocolate milk flowing from cows.
Price tags meaningless. Labels cartoons.
I won't bring a list.

Mannequins Yearning for Eye Contact

While visiting Santa Fe, which feels
a world away from my home state,
I'm disoriented tripping upon a lacuna
where monuments once stood
to honor the extermination tactics
of Diego de Vargas and Kit Carson,
and the Indian Wars, America's real
longest war. Here, the monuments
that should have been to Pueblo and Navajo
were never built, never mentioned
in the margins of my schoolyear textbooks—
Part of existence that's toppled in this new day.

Back home in Marin, the county named
for coast Miwok Chief Marin, under a sky
dimmed with fall fires, I drive west to hike
the beach trail at Abbotts Lagoon, named
for two brothers who grabbed the land
in 1858 for dairy ranching. I seek escape
from the remembrance of amended history,
eyeless busts and statues across the land
erected to glorify crimes. Their sightless gazes
akin to mannequins desperate for eye contact.

Named for a Southern Pacific Railroad
land agent who nobody seems to remember,
Redding, the town I grew up in, overlooking
the Sacramento, had cornerstones we ignored
on brick buildings from the mid-1800s,
no generals I knew of atop bronze horses.

As if to pretend that lands weren't stolen,
the first peoples weren't massacred: Modoc,
Wintu, Yana, Pit River, and Klamath River tribes.
Like there was nothing to remember.
The historic brothels and saloons have been
demolished now, transplanted by parking lots.

Away from history's rubble, at the western limit
of the continent, weight of the atmosphere
presses down on me. Sand in my face, water-doused,
I feel the collapse of seafoam.
The sweet talk of Pacific spray
trying to convince me the past won't be repeated.

To My Ocular Migraine

for Ann

So, I can pretend I'm Eve in the Garden.
A snake writhes,
winds itself into a triangular pile.
Blots my vision. No apple in sight.

No pain.
Only light.
Around the edges
an aura.

The serpent
wags like Cerberus' tail.

The onset a mystery,
the blinding spiral shimmers
in front of the world I must see.

I could be driving a used SUV.
I could be on a podium demoing software.
I could be making my kids mac and cheese.

I close my eyes and watch your movie
on my lids, starring
the familiar twitching reptile.
He just coils
and uncoils,
coils and uncoils.

It's very boring. Almost
like catechism class.

The end comes
when Satan is good
and ready.

Equipoise

My husband's pill boxes rest on the counter,
an abacus of prescriptions.
I'll remember this chapter passed down
from one ancestor to another,
weight of the family tree.
Hiatus comes from the Latin *to yawn*.
I love to ignore the gaping one.
Think *vespertine*, flourishing in the evening:
crepuscular. I crave an innocent gloaming.
Instead, I see flame-shaped markings.
Flammulated. Tattoos. Not just on owls,
the symbol of Athena.
I'm seeing too many flames.
I want to put bombed cinderblocks on mute,
erase complicity off my skin.
I want numbing for spirit pain.
Will my heart become cold like a beetle
pinned in a science project?
Launched into another grief,
my teeth hide behind the mask, the dire veil.
Let's not go back to old ways of drinking.
I mean thinking.
Give up my alibis. I must not abet.

Officers Clearing a Street Downtown

Slo-mo replay of me dusting
the bric-a-brac in the whatnot,
my cage of keepsakes.
More anti-gun protests planned
for tonight, defying curfew.
There are no phantom crimes here,
only questioning incarnations.
But trusting angels howl
in a dead language,
pronounce these words:
tutum et securum.
Safety and security.
Does my country misconstrue
our plea?
A bottle of prosecco happily
bubbles away on my table.
Opened too soon?

Beyond the Milky Way

Calla lilies in the backyard multiply
like a joyful resurgence
from loins of a lush goddess.

Wouldn't it be great to have such divine loins?
I believe I did once—wasted on youth
as the adage goes—
unappreciated for their grandeur,
the biblical proportions of such loins.

I'd nominate the loins of a goddess
to run for President.
They'd be the first-ever loins
of a goddess to be elected.

For their inauguration, the loins
would be girded in a navy pantsuit.
No, make that a backless platinum jumpsuit
and TikTok would go crazy.
Attendance would reach the moon,
even stretch beyond the Milky Way.

There'd be strict obedience to the demands
of the biblically proportioned loins
by half the people. The rest would throw
hissy fits of rebellion
like teenagers against their mothers.

Is this a yet-to-be-discovered terrestrial myth? A story
told in charcoal drawings on the walls of a sooty cave,
a titillating show of our primeval imagination.

Display of Phalaenopsis

They beckon me from the entry
of the produce aisle, queued up
as if they're hesitant to join
the serious business
of tomatoes, lettuce, and asparagus.
They seem ready to prance onstage
for the role of a lifetime.

Constrained in little ceramic pots,
their long course roots escape
from the base of hidden stems
piled with leathery, oblong leaves
shaped like rabbit ears,
as if they could hop
right off the shelf.

From the overlapping
foliage, each has a single stalk
that swans upward and holds
blooms like cancan dancers
spreading their skirts.
These merciless, coquettish
orchids tease me.

Their blooms are trying hard
to lure me, in lieu of an insect
that is beyond my understanding,
beyond any bug that exists
in this makeshift space.

Suppose I could open myself
to unfettered possibilities,
kiss these orchids
with a rouged moth mouth.

Now I'm so distracted from
my urgent list of ingredients,
I'm about to load my cart with them.
I must get ahold of myself.
Why am I here in the first place?

Technicolor Memory in Progress

I try not to think time can be bought.
This memory is a ghost matinee
produced like a low-budget western
with a crooked sheriff.
He holds belief like a six-shooter.

I'm watching an exhausting movie marathon,
bleeding worlds full of disciples.
The defacement of cities
distracts from arctic heatwaves.
Sickness distracts from the defacement of cities.
The stylish mirage of prosperity
distends its belly as the wealth gap widens.
Observatories from concrete
provide an astonishing panorama:

Streets neoned and seething,
roads run like broken capillaries.
The sky is creased with contrails,
skywritten in the names
of young Black men shot in the back,
picnicking children hit by stray bullets.

Toward a phalanx, flame flickers
like a massive lightbulb.
If only a sudden insight would go off
in the common mind of humanity.
Our eyes pinpointed, instead we're told:
Move along. There's nothing to see here, folks.

Green Rush Bonanza

How about if I spend
my weekends pretend-
prospecting the red hard-
pan of Northern California
for those caches I know
are buried there? Millions
in coins and ingots
hidden by enterprising
weed anarchists, I'm sure,
east in the Sierra Foothills
and west way up
the Mendocino coast,
banked near rocky
clay slickens and tailings,
under pine and oaken copse,
deposited by tax evaders
in nature's vault
near Sativa and Indica,
waiting for the likes of me.
Ha! Illegal green thumb,
duty-free income.

And if I took a leave
or heaved the job,
hit the road with a carload
of shovels and picks,
snuck onto those
scofflaw estates, I'd find
an illicit mother lode.
Eureka! I'd cash in

on the hidey-holes.
I'd be set for life,
rid of debt. My kids
and their kids would become
one percenters.
With my new riches I could
be a philanthropist
or a lobbyist, whatever
I desired. Although
I'd have to pack some
heat, since I fear
I would never again
trust anyone.

Farewell to Old Earth

If you stare intently, you can see
the sky seems to imprint itself
with the ever-so-faint suggestion
of the new dimension
we are sure to enter. That is,
those of us lucky enough
to be chosen for the voyage
to the vast rapturous heaven
that supplants the habitat
of Old Earth.
Creatures left behind
will be vaporized, leaving
vacant the country roads,
main streets, and weird
needle-like towers that will become
shrines to extinct civilizations.
Some of us will want to go back
to explore Old Earth,
to observe the results
of tests and projects
to save the wicked planet.
But there are those of us that don't feel
like we'll miss Old Earth.
We believe
the new home waiting for us,
cold and shiny and nice,
is full of promise.
Like all those advertised afterlives.

Dependable

Beside the stealth piano
with its keys like black licorice
so beautiful and tragic
I hear another State of the Union from a great height.
I can't even look or I might get dizzy.
I'd love to edit the world,
the geography of the mind
with its tar pit that preserves the burdens of my parents.

A brief history (of?):
<insert war/s here>
<insert denial>
<insert plague and pestilence>
<insert denial>
<insert a great leap>
<repeat>

On schedule like a bus,
here come the hand-dug graves
in grease and sorrow.
And into the firmament of its own surprise,
the latest terror
that doesn't even need to be warfare to be
terrifying.
The piano is padlocked to a stupor.

The Mystery of Antarctica's Sea Ice Has Been Solved

Fundraisers where happenings are staged
and babies kissed, flesh is pressed
like ruined leather.
The machine provides a robotic hug
to ease anxiety.

It's bad form to curse during breakfast,
everyone aglow
over the double-yoke egg.

Go ahead and keep your loose change
for the phone sex of a bygone era.
You might need it.

Glaciers calve in spectral night,
their bone-cracking din
conspiring to end all.
Thank you for the alarm
and the bond to antiquity,
obsolete geography.

An oddity of austral spring,
a hole known as a *polynya*
grows to the size of the Netherlands
(this name apt, as in sunk).

How I disdain warnings and predictions,
bury my head in new clothes.

I love my closets,
their graceless mess.

Global Positioning Systems and Healthcare

/

Tonight, the constellations guzzled
right out of the welkin, our Zodiac
gulped down a gullet. God's
digestive tract and bowels.

\\

Billions of light years from here
a planet catches the reflection of our past,
this world whirling out of the muck,
the nothing without memory
and then the something
and then

///

A protester at a die-in with a sign:
The ACA Saved My Life.
Another with: *Death by AHCA*.
When I ask what *AHCA* stands for,
I hear about preexisting conditions:
fibromyalgia, paraplegia,
ulcerative colitis
and then

\\\\

untreated
opioid addiction.

More words I can't spell.
(I ask my phone to show me a map
of places where my family could thrive.)
From now on

/////

answers to my questions
are accessible, if I pay to subscribe
to the shared intelligence ration.

The Slick Slope

My husband signs us up for Ski Patrol
and I find myself
learning CPR and how to
backboard head injuries.

I study snow conditions:
black ice, powder, Sierra cement,
the terror of tree wells.

Our children follow on their wee skis.
My husband is too fast for us
and we can never keep up.
I stay with the kids
on the bunny slope
and he schusses off
to the black diamond run.

There goes their father,
ignoring us and our cares,
zigzagging
down the fall line.

I'm only on Ski Patrol in name.
I mostly rescue the family
and sneak help behind the scenes.
Nobody sees me
when I take a drastic spill
then pick myself up again.

The Undercover Activity of Poplars

I caught them this dawn
blinking their leaves in code.

The way they touched I knew
they were exchanging intimacies.

Their fluttering entranced me,
turned pages in my brain and I entered

this pulp romance of a past lover
tumbling in oat grass. Chambray shirt

unbuttoned, me spread like a picnic,
back sticky with sap.

Then my poplars let go and tipped their crowns
in a hasty farewell when you woke up.

And I said hello to the mounting sun,
our day just swelling.

II.
Know the Dahlias

Anniversary Memento

I sleep in my clothes
so before breaking the fast
I can fetch the morning paper,
that archaic medium for news.
Then time to remove outer dead skin,
I mean shower,
the long détente
of parenting and work years gone.
Pity me expecting a bejeweled anniversary gift;
I must settle for a carafe
or crockpot. An inverse memento mori,
interlocking cells of marriage spilling.
I know my husband in our housewares.
Having brushed him with my tongue many years
during our misdemeanor home life, era
more like error, with its drugs, drinking,
and slamming of doors.
And a brief *Paradiso Terrestre*,
fleeting cataracts of Edens.
Now our routine is forgiving,
my conscience feels swaddled
and I forget anxiety,
never mind guilt,
never mind remorse
that I (we) didn't behave better
in earthly life, as I did
in my nighttime ghost life.
I cede to acceptance,
this bundle of years.

Cure Redux

High in the rafters of Earth,
a ventriloquized voice beckons
our species from the first eutherian mammal
to the Anthropocene, our hapless current epoch.
Régimes whisper to extinctions.

My mammalian body is dutiful
at its mammogram.

I am moved to tears again.
The groove in my left breast
"tissue sparing." They said, "clean margins."

What is more powerful than all
social media in its fervent
echo chamber of denials?

Who among us does not crave a cure? A miracle
like Spring's first crocus luring bees from their hives.
The science deniers reject inconvenient facts
then pray for the latest chemo when they're sick.

The Godzilla Dust Cloud

The Godzilla dust cloud from the Sahara
heads toward the southeastern corner of the U.S.,
brings gorgeous sunsets to towns in Florida and Texas.

But the cloud is feared in all the tabloids
although over millennia, this African dust
nourishes tropical islands and makes the Bahamas lush.

Was the Godzilla dust cloud on my raffle ticket?
After murder hornets, mystery fireworks, a pandemic,
and masked, marching masses like in a Bible plague?

I talk too much and bring bad news,
a mouth-wracked jukebox.
If I can't be a mum sphinx, I'll be a jabbering jinx.

That bottlebrush bush again, hue of the dust cloud's sunset.
It's grown into a tree with a million shocked filaments,
a hiding place for thieving squirrels and tree rats.

But nectar for bees and hummingbirds
(pray they show up in scorching summer).
The red stamens bleed under the bird feeders.

The tree grows and grows and costs a fortune to prune
(so let it be unruly, laissez faire).
The ladder that can't reach the top is an indictment.

Unpaid Debt

The book is a slow medium—
does a shift in the world render it implausible?
Does metaphor become literal?
The word, so light and vague, handles history
with great care, the known record of our lives fastened
to others arbitrarily at the costume jewelry counter
of life's defunct five and dime.

I might as well outrun the collectors,
my unpaid debt may expire. Run out the statute.
I might as well drink a thermos of spiked tea,
become a connoisseur of craving.
Toughened up and exuberant, the calculations flawed.

It's not church or therapy that can fix my mood.
Under nightfall, black as cormorant wings
seen through a gauzy lens there's no grief
I can't kill with a nightmare sword pointed at myself.

What did I wear in a former life?
I wear a hooded bathrobe now as I clutch
at remembrance, take a breath.
Better to fool myself and reverse what I
really fear:
the past is a frontier, the future a sanctuary.

The Shades Pulled Up and Down

1.

A gaudy omen outside my neighbor's window,
bougainvillea's flash mob of purple miniskirts.
Let autocorrect create the comic simile.
Today is like another opportunity
for sinning.

2.

The Canadian geese on a long sabbatical
from their career of migration—
they enjoy this new-found park so much
they may never go back to work.
Their maps have folded in disobedience.

3.

Enough of bad weather, the sweaty littered streets,
a single dandelion roaring at the speedsters.
I'm jealous of people who believe lead floats.
The tongues of my shoes lap at my feet.

Hewing Wood with a Darling Axe

What engines do we make?
To fish, to hunt? To destroy?
Of all our harrows, reality spangles.
I wear a mantle,
a magnetic ghost that attaches to my shoulder blades.
Sometimes brainsick
I hew wooden words with a darling axe.

Pray for the Polyphemus moths mating,
their little feet clinging to the vine.
Abdomen upon abdomen, clasped to each other,
they appear to be dead. Perhaps engaged
in a long orgasm.
Leave them in peace. They are mating.
Propagating their diurnal species,
only the two of them
so wonders will emerge with purpose,
their grubs to smell the world.

Does anyone think they could
create such a moth?
Not a robotic model.
Who among us could make a rib?
Not just whittle one.
Make the mother of us?
We cartoon our planet.

Know the Dahlias

My couch is like a plush pew.
The blankness made bearable
by a recollection of dahlias
and all their relatives invited here:
the sunflower, daisy, chrysanthemum, zinnia
lush in forgotten scat and manure
of their floriculture. Tender leaves.

How I long for clouds
of insects—
to be bothered by them
as in my childhood—
I grieve even for the gnats and no-see-ums
that used to pester us
with their swarms
on a summer evening,
the wracked spines of folding chairs,
a great ambient snore
of cars and dusk's creatures.
My limbs are stiff with reruns and solitaire.
Thoughts bloom in molasses minutes, dicotyledonous.

Mutual Denominator

Remember the time before windows were stained glass.
Before white smoke from the chapel chimney.
A scorpion suspended in amber,
the prehistoric shadows of nothing,
sheen of forever.
Unzip the chromosomes
for progeny.
What kills is never what we plan for
but I know that's false.
It's the *never* that is false.
Eyes unearthed, at least *we* (not just *I*) know
there's an end to earthliness
(humanity's mutual denominator)
in this fractured lineage of belief.
The crackle, amperage humming,
warp and gap where we celebrate
and mourn people and anything that did
and did not happen.
We all become unmothered.
I'm happy to leave suddenly
unplanned, toward dirt
waving a peace sign
at the apocalypse.
Backstage behind the velvet curtain,
the clank of a door.
This ambiguous space.
The same blink of brief.

To-do List During a Pandemic Ignored Because of Protests

The world is Monet's *Water Lilies* one day
and the next it's Goya's *Saturn Devouring His Son.*
Right after I wake up, I feel an urgent to-do list:
Learn a new lexis for isolating.
Invent an egalitarian pronoun for *we*, as in We the People.
Cocoon a realm.
Mourn the brutal death of another Black person.
Meanwhile, avoid the freeways.
Meanwhile, avoid the downtowns.
Meanwhile, avoid the smoke and mayhem down an alley.
Meanwhile, learn how to bear the unraveling.
Meanwhile, police tactics: they fire neon marking rounds
so later they find who was looting.
Meanwhile, social distancing.
Meanwhile, masses not social distancing.
On a protester's t-shirt "Nevertheless, she persisted."
Meanwhile, I feel oblivious. Who is *she?*
Meanwhile, it better be me.
Meanwhile, tweed anonymity in the Senate.
Meanwhile, we're not listening to twittering politicians.
Meanwhile, under fluorescent lights
there is a cord you pull to start the engine.
I mean the conversation.
If it breaks, use a bootlace. But try not to strangle anyone.
Meanwhile, the gash of an ATM on every corner.
Meanwhile, old newsreels act as if they are new,
new newsreels act as if they are not the same old.
Meanwhile, a pandemic
and the swing of a hospital's revolving door.

Meanwhile, mobs in masks
not because, of the virus, because of tear gas.
Meanwhile, we hunger for a vaccine
that half of us will refuse.
Meanwhile, storefronts mangled,
laptops grabbed under a sky glittering with flash bang.
Meanwhile, a makeshift memorial, bouquets and unlit candles.
Meanwhile, a white lady passes counterfeit twenties
and she is freed on her own recognizance.

Blessed Be the Calving

Forget complaints, candle-light fringed,
personal beasts muttering
like rows of folding chairs
before a concert.

I read the future in the crystal bowl
that once belonged to a grandmother.
It saw her wedding dress.
How many ambrosias since?
Sweating glaciers send postcards of themselves.
Empire's response a Panglossian hosanna:
Blessed be the calving.

Some unexpected news:
A heartburn medication may have caused
a distant relative's cancer.
They may qualify for a cash award.
As if it matters, now that their heart burns
and a tumor grows inside.

At least no ancestor of mine was left
on a doorstep (that I know of).
At least a little token of them
is not on view at the Foundling Museum,
a small charm engraved with "Mariah."
At least the tether between mother and child
was not severed, my birthright slate wiped clean.

Newspapers unfold their dated bulletins,
the placement of urgency beckons.

Scholars of nothing in particular
with their continuum of effort
fill dustbins of the internet.
Lamps still lit scorch their way to and fro
and I am awed in the slack-jawed dawn.

A [New] Context

I feel like I'm reading
the same page over and over,
checking the time
and forgetting the hour,
waving at someone
who is waving at someone else.

The drift of neurotransmitters
floats through straits, synaptic gauntlets,
this everywhere listing.
Another war blooming.
There's a moth that feeds on tears
of horses—that could be my tears
for the thought *everything is broken*.

And that we spend
twenty-six years sleeping,
seven trying to sleep.
But that's an average.
Meaningless for this day
since we (I) spend how much
doing anything meaningful.
To save our planet. For peace.

All this primordial stuff
ignored, natural and preternatural,
macro and microscopic,
the will of the Great Architect,
in regalia with tattered flags
as the virtuous minutes go.

Don't we want to fix our world.
That's not a question.

Our sighing shrines splinter
in war and weather.
Move all the statues to a museum, they say.
Move endangered mammals to a sanctuary.
Move women and children to a strange country.
Let them breathe trapped air.
Give everything dead or alive a new context.

Nepenthe

Ah Nepenthe, named for mythic nepenthe,
a drug for dispelling grief and misery—
I was introduced to this word
when I drove past Carmel on Highway 1
and stopped at the famous place once
owned by Orson Welles when he was married
to Rita Hayworth. Long ago frequented by
superstars, now just average tourists.
The restaurant's terrace overlooked
the ragged grandeur of the Big Sur coast.
I was by myself and felt shy walking past the tables
of elegant, possibly eminent, people.
I devoured an "Ambrosiaburger,"
and buoyed by optimism, went downstairs
to the chic giftshop where I got lost
in the displays of amethyst earrings,
pastel silk blouses, and pashmina shawls.
Finally, I emerged with marked-down pajamas
made of organic cotton, printed with cabbage roses
in bright shades of red, green, yellow, orange and blue.
Frida Kahlo colors, like a balm I would apply
in the evening as a sort of armor
against the day's bad news and sorrows.
At night, I changed into a woman
who hovered above molten insomnia.

Dimpled

My left breast has now become
a parody of its full and unscathed sister.
Life-saving, my left breast insists
as I slip a silicone pad into my bra.
Until this deep dimpled scar
I had hated the smooth mound
on my right shoulder,
the result of a birthmark removed.
Now I ignore that childhood disfigurement.
It could have been worse,
I'm ashamed to have complained.
My scarred breast
makes many of life's hardships
seem small,
makes me clutch each day
to my chest.
I refused reconstructive surgery,
no longer lament the little hollow bowl.
Let my body go on
in lopsidedness.
Let me compensate
for what is diminished.
The breast, even though a shadow
of itself, is still part of me,
areola and nipple intact.
This scar keeps me hitched
to gratitude
until daisies take root in my teeth.

"Dappled" Just Came to Mind

And I saw sunlight, which is so cliché
then a favorite horse from my childhood,
its coat cloud gray with raindrop circles
like splashes in a puddle.

I want to write magical realism
but I have to work hard at it.
My sentences veer back to the quotidian.
To dull descriptions and too much sense.

Can't I be thunderstruck and wake
suddenly to be a brilliant lyricist?
Be struck with rhythm
and stunning metaphors?

Or how about some startling similes?
Or subtle even, like, like …
the new rosé that's not too sweet,
just a gorgeous blush, smooth on the palate.

Oh, give me that realism sharpened
with a sorcerer's spell, realism stirred
in a cauldron with newt's eyes
and torrid wishes.

Trade my babies' milk teeth
for fairy cred? But I must hammer
my xylophone and wear earplugs
to work and slave away at Poesy.

On top of that, I'm married
to the comma,
I'm in love with punctuation.

Adam's Tag

The acute recklessness of this graffiti,
contrary hallmark all over the sidewalk,

spit and gum punctuating red zigzags
like guts spilled, pleading to be heard or ignored.

His message boils away on the garage,
on the grocery, the white van—

everywhere I look, the same handwriting—
cryptic, hard to read, stolen from a song

he couldn't imagine would be a hit,
raw lettering bled from a can:

How Does It Feel, how–does–it–feel. Words
ragged like teeth of a whipsaw.

How does it feel where God pulled your rib out?
The hole never closed properly, the rib knows

where it belongs. And now my body aches
like you're trying to escape through my womb.

Another Silence Closing In

Roses as red as a verdict
here at my right hand.
Look in my eyes, say words
to me like a fallen meteor.

The ache of it, long-ago smile,
the past undone bright as a chalice
deep enough to drown in.
Empty space in the blood
like a house foreclosed—
another silence closing in on us.

What could we have done?
As though intimacy were a signature
on a contract—
something we traded.

Listen to the sirens like a spoiled child's tantrum
on the golden street with its plate glass windows.
Kitchens of waxed linoleum,
doors with deadbolts.

Through the drapes, lawn where deer sleep.
Remember the beginning of our story,
that arc idiotic with anxiety
and lust. With lovely diction,
so beautifully pronounced.

Eyeglasses

They're lined up like little doll caskets,
my glasses cases. I went through my teens
without corrective lenses, wondered later
if impaired vision accounted for my falling asleep
every ninth sentence when reading textbooks.

Having one pair worked a couple of decades—
four eyes I was. On several occasions
men asked me to remove my glasses
and then said, "You are very attractive.
Have you considered contacts?"

I did many times, the little dents on my nose
becoming more persistent.
Now I have lenses staring at me
from all over the place: my nightstand,
the computer, near the sofa, my car.
Each for a different type of seeing—
ten eyes, you could call me.

If this keeps up, call me infinite eyes.
When I finally go, maybe I should be laid to rest
in a black, faux-alligator coffin like the case
for my designer sunglasses, the inside lining
static-free felt with my surname engraved
in gold-leaf Perpetua font.

It would have a spring hinge and I'd be draped
with a pink microfiber cleaning cloth.

For my mother's viewing the undertaker said,
Bring a pair of her glasses, she'll look more natural.

III.
Every Bit of It Mine

Every Bit of It Mine

My prairie, every bit of it mine.
The grasses, the buffalo,
the aquifers, the arrowheads,
bleached bones, prairie dogs
all are mine.
Ashes in the grate
of this country are mine.
Frayed wings of seized birds,
their absence.
The beardless face of the moon
with its stained teeth and pockmarks.
My millennium,
riches to leave my children.

"Begin the Beguine" without
singing it, without dancing.
Just "Begin the Beguine"
like my father would say
at six o'clock.
My sisters and I fussing
over dolls, over cartoons.
Mother's automation in the kitchen.
Antimacassars on the recliners
murderous for a cocktail:
rye, agave nectar, tamarind paste,
a splash of lime
over a big rock. Truly,
just discount vodka
plain, but the ice cube is real.
Bliss with a touch of deja vu.

Slant glow of the cathedral
sunset in the picture window,
the coffee table pitted
like a dart board
from kids attacking it.
In the arched proscenium,
stuffed animals:
baby rhinoceros, hyena, and zebra
trotted out with grave ceremony.
Glory above them in the shape of birth
and all its moods
snorting, laughing, braying.
What is the name of this knowledge?
"Parenthood" is inadequate.

I'm Not Really Watching Any News

Couldn't you just undress
the news lady slinked up
in her sleeveless blue shift,
the outline of her little tummy
cuteness. How I can be
distracted from all
the crime she's telling us about
by studying her lips that are
so pillowy. And
her forehead
that's weirdly smooth
above her Fuller brush
fake eyelashes.
I try to suppress
my captivation.
I don't want to undress
the weatherman
just yet.
Although, he's adorable
when he tells us we can all enjoy
the heat that's coming
our way this week.
And next. And next.
The weatherman,
upholstered
in his blue suit, is
devastating.

Hymnal

An ancient hymnal pried open over tea
in the middle of nowhere.
The country enters like a shudder.
Dry grass like matches.
Half the citizens
with their hollow vowels
have given up trying to placate the other half.
Flies swatted at settle down.
One step ahead of time,
they're swatted again.
It's an insect massacre.

Then there's my cerebral sciatica.
I fear my mind could limp forever.
What kind of mother was I
to bring children here?
The world's spate of incendiary devices, déjà vu.
This will wash over
like lipstick painted askew.
Exclamation points of sweat become
a thousand plots I cannot fathom.

Atomic clocks count down a revolution
with a note of lingerie nostalgia
staggered with an air of anxiety.
Staggered with undercover procreation.
Leadership like in a whip-crack rodeo
all twitter abracadabra.
Backwoods air full of looting blue jays.
Gingerbread dreams become drowsy and timeless,

vibrate breaths along a tangle of telephone wires,
the core of a conceivable story.

Our malls are like ziggurat ruins.
Tumults of the present on a yearning current,
the harvest moon is armed and dangerous.
There will be no body count accurate or otherwise
to make us think this battle is a game.
An innocent scuffle. Not a conspiracy.
Bombs at a distance fool us
like they're some kind of celebration.

Ah, the hymnal is an almanac.

Here's to roses the color of congealed blood, reduced to concise evidence

Somewhere between backwardness and modernity
history sweats like frozen pipes thawing.
Dogma inserts itself into justified protest,
called a battlespace by militant cops. Gonzo
far-right ideologies. Gonzo far-left ideologies.
The militia-sphere coagulates around rights, infuses
itself with the claims of conspiracy theories, a contagion
stream-sniping our lives against the background
of flourishing "flu." A police dog has a fit of coughing.
An intermittent complaint, "The crimes of the rich
are not prosecuted" mixes with grief for another
mass shooting.

Campaign buttons and tarnished coins of an empire
orphaned in my dresser drawer, the anthem
always has a wardrobe malfunction. I watch "The Thing"
remake (two and a half stars) example of a flame thrower
that never runs out of fuel. I imagine millions of couches
pointed, against ennui, to the same flickering blaze,
the isolation of our atomized lives. I'm reduced
to a flow chart on the verge of a flubbed audition
playing barber to my own hair. I've successfully become
my own bartender in the madness of this spilling allegory.
Soon I'll break out of my confines and join multitudes
(forgetting I contain multitudes).

Watersheds

Watersheds of this troubled year
drowned in the floods of panic.
Demagoguery,
a law-and-order motif.
The cultural war to get reelected.
Elmer Gantry gone wild.
You can't feel the power of this moment
on the couch.
The seraphim in one of the upstairs rooms
unshriven,
relishing our guilt.
A vanishing of nest
so hungered for a remnant of home.
A place to shelter pretty as it is
rubbing bone against bone,
working the second job.
Greed for time, for being.
It's good to meditate on beauty,
pose happy ideas.
Create tributaries of joy
in which to tread water.

The Academia I Never Had

Cars spat at the bushes along the road
past pink and green and purple houses,
the golden cables of the bridge stable
on 101 under the elbows and knees
of the fog rolling in.
An ice sculpture of words awaited me
on the job. No time for gymnasiums
or enticing perks.
Only well-ruined hips
and a sublingual pill of persistence
until deadlines slapped me
like a two-stroke engine.
I rejected academia after college
when I absconded to a corporate job,
a chain letter that kept going.
Away from daily motherhood,
my poor latchkey kiddos.
Does it matter how much
I love them now?
They were abandoned then.
And I would scrape myself home
late in the long bad commute,
disassemble in the kitchen
then drain the family to bed.

Quarry

The most magnificent hungry mouths.
The prey and my family's.
Our household of two parents,
five daughters.
I remember nature
roasted and stewed.
My father used our red nail polish
to paint the sights of his rifles.
Their gunstocks, grip and forearm,
he spent hours checkering
with cutters and fine files.
He would finish the stocks
with linseed oil and wax.
I was a kid. All I knew was
this was his craft and
he loved us
and deer hunting.

Biscotti with the Taj Mahal

I flipped through a magazine with the tip of my biscotti,
careful not to drip French roast on the page
with the Taj Mahal
while I wonder why no man ever built a temple
in my honor. Mine might be a lean-to
with a pot-bellied stove and dirt floors,
a cast iron caldron perpetually boiling bone broth.
I can feel the damp earth and sweaty windows,
not the baked white of the desert.
The gilded minarets
that I will never know.

What would I even do with such a Taj?
I would be forced to abandon my sweats,
to dress up every day in lavish silk
baring my midriff,
forced to henna my hair
and line my eyes with kohl.
Wouldn't I be forced to remain
as skinny as a fern frond?
And as delicate.

Biscotti crumbs fly onto the glossy page.
I feel I've escaped from the prison
of that Taj Mahal. I was blessed
with a humble abode,
walls that someday
might be painted robin's egg blue.

Love Story of Pears

How many times I've passed them in the produce aisle
fearful their unblemished skin conceals
blandness, disappointment.
I walk away sure they are not as good as they appear.

For the first time in our marriage, fruit trees in the backyard,
one finally revealing its identity.
In summer my day could revolve around this tree.

Pears lie on the ground each morning, with precise gnaw marks,
sharp incisors from raccoon, rat, or possum. I'm amazed
every pear tastes sweet and juicy no matter how battered
with warts, tattoos, and scratches.

The worm hole is an entrance to a sugary abode.
Fat caterpillar curled in its bed of food,
the ultimate luxury. The pears unite us
over what to do with such nourishment.

Pears fall in their circle of plenitude,
dog chasing the ones we toss into the compost.
Us trying to keep up with the bounty.

Altered

Withhold all accidents, withhold
tiny aches.
Transmogrified selves shed
from the hem of my skirt.
Streaks of feverish evening light,
demands for silence.

The sidewalk tells me something,
this asphalt church
taking the oil slick's dare:
Savor the whole fish down to its fins.
Outdo the born again.

The past, a decree.
Announced with popcorn-flavored air
like in a movie theater
with no ushers
and musty scents.
On the big screen
myself as a secular saint
or a transvestite pope,
benevolent as the gravid ocean.

Discarded incense, emptied cruets.
The shine on a tarnished crucifix.
Solid surfaces softened in waves
of latent benediction.

My small domain
a suitcase of air.

O how microscopic flecks of my skin
and my being hang midair, refuse
to fear the earthbound descent.

Swerve that hurts,
everything is a symptom.

Ephemera from a Dog-eared Almanac

Drowning is an apparent and unexpected cause
of mass mortality of common sparrows.
Ephemerals, if they avoid drought as seeds,
bloom early and in their short lives
bring brief joy under the trees.

The nun I adored when I was eight
was an arrangement in white, gray,
and black with a number 2 pencil.
I'm stuck in a power outage singing
lullabies. (No, I won't bare my breast.)

My niece says I'm the *hierophant.*
(Apologies for the weird word. And the fib.)
A lexicon or sarcoma interpreter. Am I really?
My hard work and sacrifice echo
from drugstore spectacles to common rites.

Athena places an ad in the personals
which turns into a prayer for old age,
bodies I have inhabited. Owl, wren,
replica, myth—ritual for the equinox—
descriptions of what didn't happen.

See the bird, what was luminous
before no one had music for this,
the invention of kissing.
I had a marriage in those days
because it was the thing to do.

Teatime fragments, torn pages
speaking doom and release.
The invisible (to us) shining—
the experience we are thrust into.
How to keep the flies away as long as possible.

Great Cousin Catherine

I'm thinking of you again, my namesake,
godmother to my sister, daughter of
my grandmother's sister.
Today is your birthday.

How you loved your knickknacks
from the old Stockton farm, some even worth a little:
Limoges piano trinket box, cut crystal butter dish.
Some junk: googly-eyed salt and pepper shakers,
a Depression glass candy dish.

Your closet was packed with Leslie Faye dresses
that all looked alike. Your avocado green Chevy Nova,
the engine rebuilt for the nth time, had as many miles
as your black low-heeled sandals
that you traveled the globe in those group tours.

You wouldn't dream of trading the wobbly pink chair
by your bed, the dresser with drawers that wouldn't close.
I never heard you talk about redoing anything.

Fixing what is not broken a foreign concept to you:
tearing up the kitchen with its perfectly fine
Formica and linoleum to put in granite and tile,
or installing a shower in the bathroom
with its perfectly fine clawfoot tub.

You had the same stove from 1938
and the green fridge from yesteryear,
one small step up from an icebox.

When the painters painted all your windows shut
you just opened the back door to let air in.

We knew your habits when you stayed over.
Two pieces of toast and peach jam for breakfast
every morning. And every night you slept
on a mattress as old as the hills
and as lumpy. Every night
with your bun wrapped in pink foam
shaped like Nefertiti's crown
you slept as peacefully as a queen in her tomb.

Missive to Nancy

Dear sister, you would be astonished to know that I now occupy a house (with only my husband and cat since the kids have left) which is the same architecture and plan, built the same year as that place on Santa Maria Avenue. It's a pattern house, a kit. A step up maybe from ticky tacky, a little box nevertheless. When I sit in my living room now, I imagine you shaking your crib into the hallway from our parents' bedroom where you were supposed to be sound asleep for the night per our mother's anxious prayer: *God Almighty, make baby sleep. Amen.* But, no, you would appear in the hallway at the helm of your slatted conveyance. Shaking, banging, rattling forward. Pointing to mother on the couch in front of the TV. So now I sit here and recall you in your Annie Oakley getup with six-shooter and holster. Or I see you in your highchair, bowl of cereal spilled over your head, milk dripping everywhere, our mother wiping up the mess, cussing then apologizing for words that had no meaning to her little girls who didn't have a vocabulary for what would be the design of their lives in this world.

In the Wake of My Sister

I haven't been late for my own funeral yet. I flew into my sister's late. I don't mean by airplane, I mean *flew* into the seated crowd where I was to have given her elegy, only I was late. I'd been up all night, kept up by my husband & son & daughter drinking, yelling, laughing, cursing, crammed into a room with rollaways, tripping over each other. My nagging: "Please get me to my own sister's FUNERAL on TIME." Well, memorial (since we'd already scattered her ashes on Monterey Bay where we'd gotten seasick, more than green around the gills when a whale breached in the wake of the boat). My three remaining sisters and I woozy. (*Nancy reminding us of our maiden name:* Green.) And it was after her wake I vowed I would from then on be the utmost pillar of promptness. But I am not conveying the grief that paralyzed me, her abrupt departure from us by an aneurysm, time moving in a praline-hardened sepia I could not calculate.

The Only Escape

The hiss and wake of cars on the road,
the engine dirge of trucks. Sometimes
the only escape from the noise comes
at three in the morning when my tinnitus
buzzes like electric wires. This is the silence
I know most nights. Tire dust settles
on my sheets. I'm influenced by traffic
passing my house. And days when I sit
in the back room, I'm influenced
by the bottle brush tree's looming hugeness
as it reaches toward the eaves of my house.
The din as background, communities of bees
worry at the tree, hummingbirds hover
at the red stamens. Squirrels hang
upside down from the boughs and steal
birdseed. Quail peck and scratch in the dirt.
Where can my mind go with all this distraction?

The Secrets Hidden in a Pear Tree

All my petty sins, so small,
I still think they are important
enough to admit to the pear tree
in the back yard.

I don't attend church anymore
and I've devised my own sacrament
of confession.
I took the Lord's name in vain.
I said *fuck* three times.
No one even heard me.

I carried a secret in my womb
after my second child was born.
I wanted more children. I wanted
to become pregnant over and over,
at least six more times.
I wouldn't have latchkey kids.
I'd stay home, change poopy diapers,
chase toddlers, finger paint and bake
Play-Doh all day long.

I never told anyone,
least of all my husband.
Instead, I told the pear tree
and I took the pill.

Black Walnut Tree

"… until it was home to bats and swallows"
—from Elegy for a Walnut Tree, W.S. Merwin

At my uncle's place on Clayton Road,
the "apricot ranch" we called it.
There near the old water tower it stood,
this walnut tree that shaded us
while we sorted the cots in slivery trays.

That tree was messy,
throwing down its fruit
enclosed in green spongy hulls.

John Steinbeck sat and drank wine
with my grandfather by this tree when it was young—
His brother-in-law Manny drew everyone
to this spot with his home-brewed spirits.
In the dusk, bats would feast on insects.

I remember the trilobite fossils
we dug up under the old walnut tree,
my Uncle Don telling us there used to be
a sea right where we were sitting,
and over millions of years

the earth thrust itself up,
raised the hills to the height
we know now with this walnut tree
in its second century, as it nears
the end of its prophesied lifespan
if it has not been cut down already.

To My Grandsons in the Future

You benefit today from your innocent
enthusiasm for worms, grasshoppers,
and anthills. You study foxtails
and poppies, wade in the Yuba River.

When you read this in high school,
my hope is that you are in a public one.
Well-funded, or at least with an adequate budget
for the arts. I hope your summer is still
not breaking heat records
and in winter the Yuba does not flood
causing mudslides.

Does anyone mention climate change anywhere?
(That was a *euphemism* anyway.)
Is capitalism still running *rampant*?
Does your vocabulary even include such words?
Have robots taken over the classroom?

I ask you too many questions
and I apologize. By the way,
did you know *apologia* is the root
of *apologize*? Such a beautiful word

of remorse. I can't imagine your vernacular.
I hope you do not suffer premature neck strain
from bending over your cell phones.

If you have cell phones, or know of cell phones.
Perhaps you wear a device attached to your eyes.
Perhaps you wear an embedded chip.

I digress. (Oh, I can just hear you chiding.
Grandma uses too many strange words.)

I do hope there is still a Nature you can escape to.
Where the din of machinery can't be heard.
Where artificial radiance
does not vie with the night sky.

When Wind Turbine Blades Expire

On the road over Altamont Pass
wind turbines stir by the incessant
gusts that whip through the sere grass.
The white towers form uniform rows
like the identical white headstones
where two million are interred.

When wind turbines die, their bones go
to landfill's dry catacombs. No memorial,
no eulogy for making clean energy.
Their fiberglass will never decompose
and can't be recycled.

The blades will be buried in common pits
until a startup invents a way
to chew them up into pellets or press them
for an afterlife as fiber boards.
Stacks of T. rex-sized limbs,
the remains of our good intentions.

The World Can Be a Beautiful Place

If you were born to parents
that loved you, even if
they were not-so-great parents, even if
they had little money and
worried over bills every month, if
they loved you
the world can be a beautiful place if
you got to hang around the old
aunts and uncles and your grandparents, and
the world can be a beautiful place if
your family had picnics and barbeques with
cousins and relatives and if
neighbors came over and you sat around
the yard with them and everyone and
people knocked on your door or rang the doorbell,
even strangers, and they visited or introduced
themselves and had coffee and gossiped and
laughed at the latest TV programs or played
canasta or gin rummy or even Monopoly, even if
sometimes you wished they would leave
pretty soon since it was getting late and
everyone was getting tired because they had to
go to work or school, but oh how the world
can be a beautiful place with all the people
dropping in on each other at odd times,
just coming by to see each other unannounced
and oh how everyone's faces can light up.
How the world can feel like a beautiful place.

The Kid on Holiday

You can still get a ticket for the open-air bus
that runs through El Niño torrents,
destination to be revealed after you've paid
with the lunch money of your childhood.

You might fall off at a hairpin turn
into a gutter or gully washer.
The city ignores the bus.
The suburb snubs the bus.

A storm creaks open on rusted hinges.
You think you'll get drenched.
You want the stubbornness of a deluge.
You want all hail to break loose.

It's not about you and your parents
and what happened when you were little,
though the story is pleasant
if you leave out the hard parts.

And, yes, there was a telephone.
Do you remember its rotary dial
and the short cord attached to the wall?
There was no privacy, but nothing was ever recorded.

Water spits through the gap-teeth of the world.
A cloud drools on your shoulder.
You don't even need your earbuds and galoshes
to love the piano notes of the puddle.

Novel Aloofness

Small midnight miseries
like unpaired electrons discharged
in a dialect
cruder than my mother tongue.
The good blank dirt
unquiet.
My spine lain bare as I slept.
Feeling the stems of roses
sprout an elegant
flesh turned chromium.
Alone and threadbare under the sky
of ink blue,
a magnificent hat.
No threat like in a B Mafia movie,
my bandit-masked reflection
confronted.
Root-buckled asphalt,
a mirage that shines
with a demonic gloss.
Now find myself stalled.
Each and every time, a failed attempt
to go back to how things were.
My salutation under a kind of banner,
this disguise draped across the battlements.

Garments in the Afterlife

Washed on delicate in cold water
separately. Gentle
spin cycle. Hang to dry,
preferably in shade
from a papyrus cord drawn
between the pear
and the apple tree.

The beloved hues aren't as bright
as we remember.
Some mystifying loss of their
dyed colors,
but total loss of original sin.

Which was a stubborn stain
that bedeviled many, difficult
to remove during life
so we covered it up
under layers of woolly fibs,
because we gave a fig
what people thought,
ignored the nagging
shame, reminding us
that we eat the forbidden fruit.

And our bodies,
donning their fresh clothes,
have become free
of the old tinge.
Not a trace left.

The Social Life of California Poppies

They grieve the mowed-down bunch
that fell to the gardener's weed whacker,
decide against an open casket,
petals damaged beyond recognition.

Every evening their sidewalk umbrellas
closed up, they retreat to meditations
and slumber. At dawn they unfurl
and sip juice from orange porcelain.

They crochet in a bee
with the smallest hook size,
doilies of green floss. Some of them tat lace,
the older more experienced.

They show their wares along the medians
where cars zoom by snubbing their handiwork,
taking them for granted.

They whisper to each other
their underground joke:
We know what we have.

About the Author

Cathryn Shea's debut full-length book, *Genealogy Lesson for the Laity*, is also available from Unsolicited Press.

Cathryn's poetry has been widely featured in numerous publications and was nominated for Sundress Publications' Best of the Net. Her fourth chapbook, *Backpack Full of Leaves*, was published by Cyberwit.net in 2019, and her third, *The Secrets Hidden in a Pear Tree*, was released by dancing girl press the same year. She also published *It's Raining Lullabies* with dancing girl press in 2017.

Her earlier works include her first chapbook, *Snap Bean* (CC. Marimbo, 2014). Cathryn was a 2017 Best of the Net nominee and a merit finalist in the 2013 Atlanta Review International Poetry Competition. In 2004, she received the Marjorie J. Wilson Award, judged by Charles Simic. Her poetry is featured in the anthology *Open to Interpretation: Intimate Landscape* (2012), and she has work in 2017 anthologies like *Luminous Echoes* (Into The Void) and *The New English Verse* (Cyberwit.net).

See www.cathrynshea.com.

About the Press

Unsolicited Press is based out of Portland, Oregon and focuses on the works of the unsung and underrepresented. As a womxn-owned, all-volunteer small publisher that doesn't worry about profits as much as championing exceptional literature, we have the privilege of partnering with authors skirting the fringes of the lit world. We've worked with emerging and award-winning authors such as Shann Ray, Amy Shimshon-Santo, Brook Bhagat, Kris Amos, and John W. Bateman.

Learn more at unsolicitedpress.com. Find us on X and instagram.